CONFIDENT.

EMPOWERED.

ON TOP OF MY GAME!®

D1104951

How to WIN as the CEO
of Your Life and Business.

WRITTEN BY

NECOLE PARKER

Published by
Live Limitless Authors Academy & Publishing Co.
Publishing@sierrarainge.com
www.livelimitless.co

Necole Parker Contact Information:
Website: www.ceonecole.com

Email: info@ceonecole.com
Printed in the United States of America
Cover Design by: Adam Wade

ISBN: 978-1-952903-16-8

Library of Congress Control Number 2021910425

DEDICATION

This book is dedicated to every woman who was told that she would not succeed. To every woman who has had to pursue her dream in the face of adversity; those who have discovered the true transformative power of mustard seed faith. May you always be reminded that anything is possible.

Confident. Empowered. On Top of My Game! ®

ACKNOWLEDGEMENTS

To my grandmother who always told me to never give up and to paddle my own canoe.

To my parents, Michael and Jacqueline Parker, who instilled in me that I have the power to be anything I want to be and to never allow anyone to tell me any different. I will forever honor and cherish the time, love, and wisdom that they have deposited into me throughout the years.

To my siblings, Kim, Michael, and Kelli, who taught me that sibling rivalry prepares us for the world, and above all, that family will always come first.

To my amazing son, Jordan, I love you beyond words. God has no limits on what He can do in your Life. Keep dreaming, thinking, and living *big!* I am so very proud of who *you are!*

To my grandkids, Jayden and Jordynn, you are brilliant beyond words. God has something great in store for your lives. I am happy and blessed to call you my grandkids.

TABLE OF CONTENTS

INTRODUCTION

"Quit and create your own," are the words that echoed across the room after I found myself complaining to my father for the last time about the inequalities, gender disparities, and lack of representation that I experienced working in a male-dominated industry. The words rang out from my father's mouth with a sense of urgency that I still remember to this day. I don't know if his tone was a result of his frustration with the mistreatment that I was enduring, or if he was flat out tired of hearing me gripe about a system that was resistant to change no matter how much I had proven my worth through client and contract acquisition.

I was thirty-six years old, drowning in $75,000 of debt as a result of a failed marriage, and my current residence was the comfort of my parents' basement. At first, the thought of quitting seemed illogical and downright out of the question. Yet, as I sat with the heaviness of feeling inadequate in the face of my best work, plus the conviction of my father's stern advice, I knew that the burden of my begrudged position at the small, male-dominated real estate advisory group firm where I was employed would only get heavier. The disdain that I was dealing with would come down to a decision. The surety that resounded in my father's expression when he encouraged me to walk away from a company where I was carrying 70 percent of the revenue hit me like a ton of bricks.

If I'm being honest, my vexation extended beyond being consistently overlooked for promotions for which I was overqualified. My contempt could not be completely captured in the injustices that I often encountered as a black woman who was audacious enough to climb the corporate ladder. The indignation that I felt could not be limited to the many black sheep moments that I experienced in the boardroom; it was deeper than that. I was fed up with giving my all to relationships, opportunities, and employers that did not have the capacity to honor my worth. I was done settling and no longer willing to accept less than what I knew I deserved. I was living in a basement, navigating the disappointment that accompanies divorce, teeter-tottering between the depths of depression and the heights of hope, while working to shatter the barriers that too often cage and undervalue the underrepresented. I was existing between the reality of where I was, and the dream of where I desired to be. I was meddling in the middle of "nothing to lose" but "everything to gain," and it was during that rock bottom moment that I realized that whatever I wasn't changing, I was actually choosing.

Fighting my fears and resisting the tears that were welling in my eyes, I knew that I had come to a crossroad in my life that required a version of me that had not previously existed.

Shedding the old shell of myself required me to upgrade the standards of my self-worth and home in on my time, while honoring my talent. I had to position myself unapologetically on the starting lineup while refusing to lose or allow anyone to place me on the sideline. I was no benchwarmer, role-player, or mascot. I was a woman who was willing to work for the win that I wanted, and although it appeared as if I was down for the count, the transformative truth was that the ball was in my court.

That night, I drafted two formal letters to submit to my employer. One was a resignation letter putting them on notice that I was setting sail and becoming the captain of my own ship. The other was a consultant agreement that outlined how I would complete the current projects that I was already working on while articulating the rules of engagement once those projects were completed. You see, I was responsible for the majority of the company's revenue. Although they had failed to adequately embody the essence of diversity and inclusion during my tenure, they were business savvy and knew that it was in the best interest of their fiscal forecast to oblige with my terms. They signed the consultant agreement, and I walked out of that meeting with my first client as an entrepreneur and a newfound sense of confidence, empowerment, and possibility.

It was in my parent's basement that I made a multi-million-dollar decision that changed the trajectory of my life. I desired and deserved more. So, I decided that I was done waiting for anyone to give it to me. I was tired of working hard and hoping that someone would realize my worth. I was no longer seeking validation, approval, or a seat at the table. I was building my own table and taking a chance on change. Out of all the things that I had lost, my faith remained unrelenting, and my will to win never faltered.

I know what it's like to bear the bruise of navigating between a rock and a hard place. I understand the stress and struggle of starting over; I've lived through the pain of living beneath my potential, and I've tossed and turned at night, wrestling with the affliction of rejection.

Today I am the CEO of a multi-million-dollar, full-service program and project management firm boasting numerous federal government and commercial clients like Coca-Cola and many other Fortune 500 companies. My office is a 6,000 square foot state of the art facility that employs more than fifty-five people. But before I was a successful CEO, I was a woman who dared to dream and had the discipline to do the work, to believe and to execute; a woman who learned from her mistakes and leveled up from her losses.

Before I was able to acquire 50 million dollar contracts in my business, I had to first accept that my personal and professional growth would be a result of my resolution to stop playing second-best and shrinking back. I had to hold space for myself so that I could show up and shine like never before.

There are no words to fully encompass the joy and fulfillment of betting on yourself and subsequently winning big! You deserve to experience the thrill of visualizing and materializing the life of your dreams. You owe it to yourself to dream big, think big, win big, and live big. There is no honor in living small, just regret and missed opportunities.

You're peeling back the pages of this book because there is something deep within you that is begging to be birthed. The discomfort that you fight against day in, and day out is a clarion call that you've outgrown where you are and it's time for you to shift. Perhaps you're not tired, just uninspired by work and relationships that don't serve you. Maybe you're working your nine-to-five and you're finally ready to make your side hustle your main gig. Maybe you're a small business owner who can't seem to hit your revenue goals because your current prices are a sad reflection of your personal value assessment. Maybe you're a mom failing to find balance, and you desperately desire to seek harmony in your life by focusing on your priorities and the things that fulfill you. Maybe you're living in a basement, sleeping in your car, or in between work, and while your current conditions are less than desirable, you know deep down that the promise on your future is one of power, purpose, and prosperity.

I wrote this book with you in mind. As you turn each page, my desire is that you conquer the currency of confidence, be empowered to live life on your own terms and embark on a total life transformation that allows you to live life at the top of your game. This book is an authentic and unapologetic guide to help you WIN as the CEO of your life and business.

Chapter 1

GET YOUR HEAD
IN THE GAME!
Developing a CEO Mindset

———— • ✸ • ————

"You're not born a winner or loser;
you're born a chooser. So, choose to
work hard and win!"
~Necole Parker

I t's been said that winning is based on how you perform in the final quarter. It's not always a matter of how you start; sometimes victory is determined by how you show up when it matters the most. Too often, we find ourselves living beneath our potential, repeating cycles, and staying stuck simply because we have yet to make a life-changing choice. Our decisions are the greatest determinants of our future; our lives act as a mirror to what we've chosen to accept, believe, and act on.

I was working in the basement of my parents' home when I earned $1,000,000 for the first time. Although my conditions weren't desirable, I knew that the discomfort that I was experiencing was temporary. I refused to make and act on decisions that didn't serve my growth. I felt like I was at my lowest point, but I knew that I wasn't going to stay there. I had every reason to wallow in pity; after all, I was divorced, in debt, and displaced. To be honest, there were several moments that brought me to my knees in prayer.

There were even times when I've had to sit with doubt, wrestle with frustration and affirm my beliefs in what was possible. Yet, while I endured the aches of hardship, I couldn't escape the emotions that accompany the process of sad endings. I held onto hope for new beginnings. I could have spent time and energy being bitter, blaming myself, blaming my ex, blaming God, or replaying failed scenarios; but I made a decision to do something different in my life. I decided that I was no longer waiting on anyone to bet on me. The cards were in my hand, and I was finally going to play to win.

Get past the mistakes that you may have made. Forgive yourself for choosing things that did not reflect your worth and decide that since you're still in the game. Winning is still possible. In fact, decide that winning is the only option and then commit to the work, the effort, and the fortitude required to accomplish greatness—because that's what winners do!

Entrepreneurship is a sacred journey of self-discovery. Most CEOs and small business owners would agree that the process is a path of personal development. Much of what you learn along the way become steppingstones that elevate you to new levels. Those who achieve their goals and are awarded the benefits of believing in themselves have been able to build from things that have gone wrong. We gain more from our losses when we choose to learn from them.

I have traveled the world speaking and sharing insight on effective business strategies, leadership, mentorship, and the wins and woes for women working in government contracting and other corporate entities. I am often asked how I've been able to acquire success. When I reflect on this question, I realize that there are few things that individuals who have decided to disrupt the normal and resist the status quo of society have in common: We all believe that we can win! It boils down to the caliber and the quality of your mindset.

Today, I am recognized as a highly successful chief executive officer. I launched my project management and consulting firm in 2007, and since its inception I've acquired over 140 million dollars and counting in contract revenue to date. Being a CEO is more than a glamorized title that you promote on your social media feed. It's a declaration of results driven decisions—a lifestyle of trial, error, and execution. It has everything to do with your capacity to manage problems, create resolve, and navigate conflict.

A CEO is the highest-ranking executive in a company or organization. Their primary responsibilities include making major decisions; managing overall operations and resources; and acting as the visionary, executioner, and chief communicator.

A CEO is a leader! They know how to manage people, expectations, emotions, and outcomes. So, whether you're running a company, managing a home, or simply taking charge of your life, developing a CEO mindset will prove to be beneficial and incredibly effective in empowering you to win, lead and level up in your life.

A CEO has many functions. They are similar to an athlete who is fearless, focused, and relentlessly trying to score the winning point during the last quarter of the game. They are like a mother, in a way, who is tasked with the operational functions of coordinating dinner, laundry, and soccer games. An effective CEO is a leader who executes.

When presented with a problem, leaders focus on solutions. They commit to the vision, and they do what is necessary to achieve their desired outcome. For a player attempting to make a final bucket before the sound of the buzzer, it's about daring to make that unlikely shot in the heat of the moment. For the mother managing the needs of her home, it's about understanding the needs of those you've been called to serve; and for C-suite executives it's about making decisions that benefit the company's bottom line.

How you win is a reflection of how you think.

CEO MINDSET PLAYBOOK

- Be Clear about Your Goals!

  You can't hit a target that hasn't been established. If there is no vision for success, how will you know when you've achieved it?

- Understand the Value of People!

  When you can identify the strengths of those around you, you are able to position individuals accordingly.

- Focus on Winning!

  Visualize the best possible outcome, and then make sure that your actions, your beliefs, and your words align with that vision.

- Stop Downplaying Your Failures!

  If you're afraid to fail, you may lack the capacity to manage winning on a massive level. If you're not making mistakes, you're not playing a big enough game. Resilience is the by-product of experience. You'll never truly know the thrill of scoring a game point if you're too afraid to leave the bench. Scuffed knees, finger jams and sprained ankles are just indicators that you are indeed in the game. The bench may present itself as a safety zone, but you have to hit the court to win the game.

Take a moment to examine your own beliefs, core values, and overall outlook in life. Do your actions align with the things that you are asking for? Where do you spend your time? Your money? Your focus?

When you're presented with a problem, do you dwell on what's going wrong? Or do you assess the situation in an attempt to discover a solution? Those who have a CEO mindset are able to recognize opportunities when faced with opposition.

Create your own CEO playbook. Be bold enough to visualize the life that you want and then take it a step further and write it out! Get very clear about what you want, and then figure out who you need to become, what habits you need to break, what decisions you need to make, what changes you need to implement, what relationships you need to release, and what resources you need to leverage in order to materialize the life that you've visualized.

Create your game winning strategy and then wake up every day and choose thoughts, people and things that bring you closer to that victory. You deserve to live a life that you love. That "out of this world" idea that you're afraid to embrace is waiting for you to finally take action so that it can manifest. You are a winner, and winning is what you've been designed to do. You have the grit and grind to achieve on a large scale. You don't have to settle for what life hands you, you can go against the grain, you can extract purpose from pain. All of this is possible; you just have to **_get your head in the game_**!

Chapter 2

THE MENTORSHIP MANTLE
Being an Example of Excellence

———————— • ✻ • ————————

"Mentoring is a brain to pick, an ear to
listen and a push in the right direction."
~ *John Crosby*

The right mentor can completely shift the trajectory of your life. Mentors offer insight, foresight, guidance, wisdom, accountability, and support with problem-solving. A good mentor has been where you are, and they have made it further down the road, presenting themselves as a pathway to possibility. They motivate, inspire, and role model. They act as an example of success and can provide invaluable knowledge, access to resources, and advocacy for their mentees.

Success is rarely accomplished in a silo. Instead, progress is often a measure of the people you surround yourself with and the voices that shape and influence both your intrinsic narrative and your personal perspective. Having the right people in the realm of your reach is key.

Carla Harris is the vice chairman, managing director and senior client advisor at Morgan Stanley. In her TED talk, she discusses what she has coined "Relationship Currency." It's the currency that is generated by the investments that you make in the people in your environment. This concept highlights the correlation between the relationships you cultivate and the value that you gain by leveraging your personal influence. What I appreciate most about this philosophy is that it demonstrates the importance of making deposits in the lives of those around you.

Relationships are like plants: in order to thrive they must be nurtured. In order for your relationships to serve you, you must also be able to provide a value exchange. This can be through "frequency of touch"—the act of increased familiarity through consistent or continued connection with those in your environment—educating those around you, creating and leveraging opportunities for others, or by simply serving a need or solving a problem. The problem solvers of the world are the highest paid and the most celebrated because people invest in solutions. This is why I always tell my mentees to enter into relationships with the understanding that reciprocity is the fuel that drives genuine connections.

Authentic associations are bridged by the bond of clear communication, respect, and managed expectations, and they are mutually beneficial. You may not always be able to give someone exactly what they've been able to give you, but it is wise to examine how you can serve them in a way that adds value to their lives.

For instance, a mentor's role is to guide and support their protégé, but the mentee cannot be an inactive participant in the relationship. There are things that are required of a mentee that are critical in creating a healthy and impactful exchange. A good mentee is one who is clear about their goals and needs. They are respectful of their mentor's time, take accountability for their own progress, and are coachable and willing to learn. While it is evident how a mentor adds value to their mentee, it's important to consider how the same can be true the other way around; after all, the best relationships are a two-way street, or what I like to call a win-win.

A mentee can exhibit value to their mentor by providing them with feedback on their leadership style. There is a sense of fulfillment that is gained from giving someone advice and then witnessing them reap the rewards. Mentees often get to know their mentors up close; this is an opportunity for them to find a need in their mentors' lives and discover a way to fill it. It can be as simple as noticing that while your mentor is a savvy business professional who dominates in the boardroom, they are completely incompetent when it comes to establishing social capital in the digital world. They may be unstoppable in their negotiation tactics, but easily stumped when trying to navigate the algorithms of social media. Offering them support that helps articulate their brilliance online is just as valuable as them showing you how to diversify your portfolio. Both efforts contribute to enhancing of the other party.

There is no arguing that mentors are a crucial key to advancement, but you may find yourself asking, "How do

I get one?" The truth is, it's not always as easy as one would think. I remember being rejected by a woman whom I admired. When I requested that she take me under her wings, she declined. Of course, I was disappointed, and I'd be ingenuine if I said I wasn't a bit surprised. This was a woman whom I had worked with and learned from. I'm not sure why she refused my request, but what I know for sure is that taking responsibility for someone else's success should never be taken lightly.

Stepping into someone's life as a guide on their growth journey should be a decision that one makes with consideration for one's capacity to serve. A mentor should be able to provide their mentee with time, attention, and communication in order to be most impactful. Carrying the role of a mentor is the embodiment of a life-changing mantle. It's an interest and investment into the personal or professional evolution of someone whom your experience, skillset, or knowledge best serves. It's a distinguished role that serves as an example of excellence.

Research suggests that there are seven different types of mentors. University of the People (www.uopeople.edu) specifically defines these seven mentor archetypes as:

1. **The Experienced Leader:** In a professional setting, this is someone with high status and seniority who has made their way up the ranks. They have gained enough personal experience and knowledge to impart it to those who are up-and-coming stars. They can form a mentorship relationship with their apprentices or through a formal mentorship program in the workplace.

2. **The Coach:** The coach may be a mentor that the HR department has brought in or a consultant. Often, this type of life coach is employed by those who may be making a career change or have personal goals that they need help to achieve.

3. **The Educator:** Teachers often become mentors who work with their current or prior students. They may become a mentor informally by helping to guide students during office hours or it could be a sanctioned relationship by the administration.

4. **The Self-Help Type:** People can also find mentorships in written words or lectures. This may come in the form of self-help books, manuals,

articles, websites, and more that offer advice on how to learn and grow.

5. **The Inner Mentor:** In some cases, you could be your own mentor. When you listen to your own gut and intuition, it could bring to light the answers you're looking for. This could come from leaning on your past experiences or identifying the reasons why your situations are the way they are.

6. **The Trusted Listener:** Some mentors are great listeners. With their active listening techniques, they make sure you feel heard and may be a sounding board for your own ideas.

7. **The Peer Provider:** Within school settings or organizations, you may befriend a peer who turns into a mentor. This could involve the benefit of sharing networking contacts and offering support for one another.

These are the various ways that mentorships are categorized. It's important to know where and how you fit in this model.

Outside of mentorship, there are other relationships that serve as catalysts for personal and professional advancement. They are sponsors and advisors. The distinguishing factor between a mentor and a sponsor is a matter of money. While a mentor invests time, energy and wisdom, a sponsor is more centered around investing capital and physical currency to aid in your development. This can be by paying for tuition or other forms of training, funding a business idea, or covering expenses for living. An advisor is someone who helps you to evaluate your goals, realize your potential, refer you for opportunities, and empower you through education and insight.

Having the right people in your life, who are properly positioned in how they serve a need, exhibit strength, solve a problem, create convenience, or increase fulfillment in an organization, contributes to success. The same fundamentals can be applied to your family structure and your personal relationships. Whether you're building a team or working to prioritize peace and efficiency in your life, there are a few things that are "tell-tale" signs that you are synergizing with the right people—the people who are best for you do what they say they will do. They are impeccable with their word, and you find that you can depend on them. They support you. They celebrate your growth, and they share your core values. You may not always agree on politics or who deserved to win the Grammy for the record of the year, but when it comes to the caliber of character and integrity, you are aligned.

Alignment can be more effective and beneficial than hustle. Simply being in the right place at the right time, with the right people can elevate you higher than grinding to get ahead. True alignment is the frequency of being in agreement with a person, group, party, or cause. The momentum of like minds and common goals is a catalyst for elevation.

You need to get clear about what you want out of life and then decide who the key players are that will contribute to your growth.

Examine your areas of weakness and then be intentional about building relationships with those who are strong where you may be lacking.

Use this guide below to create a winning playbook to identify and position your people.

THE POWER OF THE PEOPLE PLAYBOOK

1. What are your desired areas of growth?

    Financial goals, personal goals, fitness & health goals?

    _____

    _____

    _____

    _____

    _____

2. What are your strengths? What do you do well? What are your gifts and talents? What can you bring to the table?

    _____

    _____

    _____

    _____

    _____

3. Where are your weak spots? Who is strong in areas where you lack? How can you connect with them? Are they online? Do they have a private Facebook group, coaching program or free offer through their mailing list? Is there a void that you can fill for them?

_____

_____

_____

_____

_____

4. Why are your goals important? What can you look forward to after achieving your goal?

_____

_____

_____

_____

_____

5. Who are the five people that you engage with most often?

    1.

    2.

    3.

    4.

    5.

6. How do they enhance your life? Do they drain you or inspire you? Can you grow with them? Do you learn from them? Does the relationship align with your core values and future goals?

    _____

    _____

    _____

    _____

    _____

7. Who are the five types of people that you need in your life right now and why?

Do you need a therapist? Mentor? Advisor? Life Coach? Friend? Accountant? Brand Strategist? Assistant?

_____

_____

_____

_____

_____

When you're clear about what you need, you are able to eliminate the headache of delay that comes with being distracted by the wrong relationships.

Develop Your Relationships and Lean on Your Inner Circle

I believe that people should always position themselves by cultivating relationships and growing their inner circle. My mentor, Dr. George Fraser, taught me to connect with others by serving them. One impactful lesson he taught me is that you should ask questions such as, "How can I serve you? How can I get educated by you? What can I do to give back to you?" Cultivating relationships through serving others has worked for me because it helped me get my foot into doors that were otherwise closed.

A key is to identify and target people with whom you wish to develop a relationship and then build and leverage those relationships by serving on their committees, participating in their community events, giving back, donating to their causes, providing transportation when they are in town, and being in their network of support. This is a sure strategy to add value to them and to also learn from them along the way. People want to get in because they want to fit in, stay in, or obtain some type of benefit, but you must leverage and nurture the relationships properly.

Unfortunately, all too often, people will try to pull, pull, pull and take, take, take. There has to be an intrinsic value that you are offering that speaks to the person with whom you are trying to build a relationship. Otherwise, your attempts will be in vain. I encourage you to add value and remember that nobody owes you anything.

Mentors are key! They provide you with the good, bad, and the ugly, both personally and professionally. They give it to you in the realest and the rawest ways. Leaning on your mentors helps you stay calibrated and grounded. Sponsors and advisors advocate for you professionally. They know you. They understand you, and they campaign for you.

The relationships in your life are your human capital. Human capital is the hardest resource to manage as a business owner. This is a truth that most executives hold. When I engage with my social media audience online, like most content creators, we are more inclined to post our highlight reel. We delight in the thrill of sharing our wins, but on the other side of that are the challenges that high achievers face behind the scenes.

Managing people, expectations, and relationships has been a consistent learning curve for my team and me. As project management, delegation, remote work, and global conditions have dramatically shifted, there is a lot to understand when it comes to hiring new employees and contractors. Commitment and consistency are tough to find in this fragile economy, which makes me extremely grateful for my current team members. Having the right people on board creates efficiency and increases productivity.

Who are the people in your industry, your network, or your sphere of influence who can help you maximize your potential? Seek them, honor their work and spend time learning from them. Position yourself among people who add value and prepare you to *win!*

Chapter 3

THE REPUTATION FACTOR
Protecting Your Brand Promise

————— • ✹ • —————

"Do not leave your reputation to chance
or gossip; it is your life's artwork, and
you must craft it, hone it, and display it
with the care of an artist."
~ *Robert Greene*

Outside of relationships, your reputation is one of your most valuable assets. Your reputation is a reflection of how others perceive you. In business, your reputation is a repertoire of your brand promise. It includes the products and services that you deliver and how your customers engage with your business. Managing public perception while guarding the character and integrity of who you are and what you do is a matter of business preservation and relevance maintenance. Companies understand the importance of monitoring and managing how their audience, customers, community, competitors, and network feel toward their business and performance. This is why customer support and customer satisfaction are top priorities for any business with a desire to sustain and scale their company.

Firms that possess positive reputations tend to attract better people, and they are perceived as being able to provide more value than their counterparts. Their customers tend to be more loyal which increases their brand equity.

I have been fortunate in my career to have been able to benefit from many opportunities that have allowed me to ascend to new levels. Many of the opportunities that I have been able to take advantage of came by word-of-mouth. How people experience you and the quality of service you deliver directly impacts your next opportunity. This is why it's critical that you always maintain a standard of excellence in everything that you do. You never know how one project, one deal, or one client will lead to many more.

Integrity is a mirror of your ethical standard, and how you align your conduct with your core values and beliefs.

I was raised to be impeccable with my word, to keep my promises, and to always make good on the things I commit to. After my divorce, I was left to pay off $75,000 of past debt as well as provide $40,000 of college tuition for my son. I lived with my parents for four years until I paid the debt off in full. I refused to take on any new commitments until I was able to satisfy my current obligations. Having a good credit path was part of my value system. A credit score is an indicator of integrity, and it's a compass for how well you keep your word and manage your resources. On top of my desire to eliminate debt, it was imperative that I maintained a positive credit history in order to keep the security clearances necessary for government contracting. You see, reputation plays a huge role in how others deem you worthy of partnerships and opportunities.

After I embarked on my entrepreneurship journey, I was able to maintain working relationships with the companies and organizations that I had previously worked for. Most of my employers became my sub-contractors, and

I'm certain it was due in large part to the reputation that I had earned. Even today, the majority of my contracts are by referral. When you show up and serve in excellence, the reward is increase.

C-suite executives identify reputational risks as one of the most debilitating threats to business. A poor reputation can disrupt market capital and leave company leadership in disarray. Whether you're running a Fortune 500 company or a small business, it is wise to understand reputational risk and how to effectively manage it.

Reputational risk is defined as the potential for negative publicity or uncontrollable events to have an adverse effect on a company's revenue or public perception. I've included a risk assessment sheet on the following page to help you measure your current performance.

Confident. Empowered. On Top of My Game! ®

REPUTATION RISK ASSESSMENT

Rate yourself NI (Needs Improvement), MP (Making Progress), NS (Need Support), W (Winning). In every area you're not winning, commit to whatever is necessary to score a win in that category.

Quality of Services	NI	MP	NS	W
Company Leadership	NI	MP	NS	W
Employee Retention	NI	MP	NS	W
Culture of Company	NI	MP	NS	W
Community Engagement	NI	MP	NS	W
Media Narrative	NI	MP	NS	W
Brand Alliances	NI	MP	NS	W
Competitors	NI	MP	NS	W
Company Vision and Core Values	NI	MP	NS	W
Company Position on Politics and Social Issues	NI	MP	NS	W

Chapter 4

CASH & CARRY
The Worth & Work
of a Powerful Woman

———————— • ✺ • ————————

"Know who you are. Know what you
want. Know what you deserve.
And don't settle for less."
~Tony Gaskins

The culture of Corporate America, along with its history of missing the mark when it comes to holding space and honoring the contributions of women and people of color, is a mirror image reflecting the prevalence of an unbalanced power structure. Simply put, if women and minorities want to even the scale against their white male counterparts, then there needs to be an increase of representation on their part. We need more black women and underrepresented demographics in leadership roles with decision-making capabilities.

I remember being up for a promotion that I believed I was a great fit for. During that time, the company I was working for had hired a younger white woman, and I had been tasked with the responsibility of training her. Imagine how disheartened I was. She had just come onboard with the company and was able to surpass me and climb the corporate ladder; although, in my opinion, I was more qualified, more competent, and more capable. This wouldn't be the only time I've had to give myself the "Don't Cry" speech in order to save face and preserve my dignity. As a woman working in a white-male-dominated industry, the ability to unapologetically take up space is a muscle that you learn to flex. You must be an advocate for your equity while also prioritizing professionalism.

During the closing of one of my proudest contract acquisitions, I can recall showing up to the meeting and being halted at the door while my male counterparts were granted access to the meeting room. This was another one of those "Don't Cry" moments where I had to master my emotions and hold back tears. I stood puzzled at the door as it was closing in my face. I was a bit paralyzed in the face of rejection. Before I could express a response, the client whom I had acquired noticed that I was being refused entry into the boardroom. He immediately addressed the woman who was acting as the door guardian and advocated on my behalf.

He spoke out and stated that it was only right that I have a seat at the table since I had been the one to bring the deal to the table in the first place. The woman at the door reluctantly granted me entry but went on to instruct that I sit in the back of the room and not at the table among my peers. As I sat in the rear of the room, I realized that no matter how much value I added to the company, there were still too many people who questioned whether or not a black woman deserved a seat. That was a turning point in my career.

I was eventually offered a lower tier promotion at the company. It came with an immediate 7 thousand dollar bonus. I accepted the bonus and then turned in my resignation. This "Cash and Carry" maneuver was a clear demonstration of my frustration with being asked to sit in the back of the room. Make no mistake, women deserve to be seated out front. Not only are we competent, but we are qualified and capable. Consistently being undervalued in the organizations that I served forced me to reassess the work that I was giving so much of myself to and the worth that I assigned to it.

During a conversation with one of my superiors after my resignation, he confessed to me that the reason they had decided not to promote me was because some of the issues that the company was facing were not suitable to be handled by a woman. I paused and then proceeded to tell him, "If a woman had the opportunity to lead, then many of those same issues would fail to exist in the first place." As he worked to wrap his mind around the truth-bomb that I had dropped, I smiled with a sense of assurance, knowing at that moment, I had made the right decision to walk away from that position. If the worth and work of a powerful woman was going to be celebrated, it would be on her own accord, and I was okay with that. It's been over thirteen years, and I'm still leading and building to the beat of my own drum.

Some experiences show up in our lives to create enough discomfort to force us to make a life-changing decision. The right decisions make way for elevation while the wrong decisions cause you to repeat the lesson. As I climbed to new heights of success, I learned that the higher the mountain, the thinner the air. As you go up, you grow in awareness of the resources necessary to help you survive increased altitudes. Properly assessing the worth of what you offer in any environment is not just a great tool to earn more money, it's also necessary for your survival.

PERSONAL AND PROFESSIONAL
VALUE ASSESSMENT

Take a moment to measure your performance in each category listed below. List out your accomplishments, goals and needs in each category. When you get clear about your values and your limitations, you can make deliberate and intentional decisions that will contribute to your success.

Education

_____

_____

_____

_____

_____

_____

_____

_____

_____

_____

_____

Experience

_____

_____

_____

_____

_____

_____

_____

_____

Capacity to Solve Problems

_____

_____

_____

_____

_____

_____

_____

_____

_____

Social Equity

_____

_____

_____

_____

_____

_____

_____

_____

Financial Literacy

_____

_____

_____

_____

_____

_____

_____

_____

_____

Self-Esteem

_____

_____

_____

_____

_____

_____

_____

_____

_____

Confidence

_____

_____

_____

_____

_____

_____

_____

_____

_____

Accomplishments

_____

_____

_____

_____

_____

_____

_____

_____

_____

Organizational Memberships

_____

_____

_____

_____

_____

_____

_____

_____

_____

Community Ties

_____

_____

_____

_____

_____

_____

_____

_____

_____

Chapter 5

A FRACTION
OF FORTITUDE
Implementing the 80/20 Rule

———— • ✳ • ————

"Be thankful for what you have;
you'll end up having more. If you
concentrate on what you don't have, you
will never, ever have enough."
~Oprah Winfrey

Although my parents conceived me during their teenage years, they were mature and wise enough to instill life enhancing principles into me during my upbringing. One principle that has stuck with me throughout the years is the 80/20 quotient. This is a measure of effort, execution, and performance. My parents taught me that in life, it would be necessary to equalize mistakes, setbacks, and disappointments by turning my failures into success. I have always been a high achiever and my parents have always maintained an expectation of excellence for me. While I always aim for the highest target in every corner of my life, I've come to learn that much like balance, perfection is an illusion.

It's unrealistic and incredibly unfair to think that you will always get it right 100 percent of the time. As part of being human, we all have a predisposition to encounter some errors along the way. If you're an ambitious woman of action like me, then you, too, have set incredibly high standards for your own performance. Although it's admirable to aim high, it's equally important to have a system to adequately gauge your glory. This is where the 80/20 rule comes into play.

When you quantify the caliber of your work, 80 percent of your goals or milestones should meet or exceed your expectations. Twenty percent represents the ratio of things that require more attention, more effort and more growth. The sum total of the things that are being calculated should be an all-inclusive list of the things in your life or work that demonstrate your priorities and model that which fulfills you; and you must aim to never fall below the 80 percent marker.

How do you rank the roles and responsibilities in your life? What is most fulfilling to you? Is it being a mom? Or being a boss? Does hitting your revenue goals drive you more than tackling the to-do list of your home? Do you value quality time with close family and friends or sacred moments or personal seclusion? This is where complete honesty is mandatory. You must be completely truthful when designing your list of priorities and personal fulfilment. This is an articulation of what's important to you and what fuels you. If your list is not ripe with truth, it will fail to communicate how you measure up.

80/20 Assessment

Use this tool to get clear about how your values measure up. What categories contribute to your 80 percent rank? These are the areas where you score the highest. The categories where you rank the lowest represent your 20 percent.

Rank yourself accordingly. 1= I am not satisfied with my performance or effort and I could increase my focus in this area. 5= I've made progress in this area but could still increase my efforts to increase personal fulfillment. 10= I am committed to this area in my life and I am satisfied with my performance and effort.

1. Personal Obligations   1 5 10

2. Health and Fitness   1 5 10

3. Financial Wellness   1 5 10

4. Goal Achievement   1 5 10

5. Satisfaction in Relationships 1 5 10

6. Growth and Development   1 5 10

7. Business Goals   1 5 10

8. Family   1 5 10

9. Vision for the Future   1 5 10

10. Fun   1 5 10

Chapter 6

BE THE CEO OF
YOUR OWN HAPPINESS
Designing a Life That You Love

——— • ✳ • ———

"Sometimes happiness is a feeling, and
then sometimes it's a choice."
~Necole Parker

Don't ever doubt the power that you possess to create a world that you enjoy living in—it comes down to a matter of choice and inspired action. I've worked with women who couldn't determine whether or not they were truly happy simply because they had never taken the time to define or design happiness through their own lens. When we fill our lives with things that we think will bring us joy, we inadvertently take up space with untested ideas of bliss instead of tried-and-true testaments of inner thrill. You owe it to yourself to distinguish what makes you feel most alive. Otherwise, you're merely existing—never truly living a life that mirrors your wildest dreams. Know that you deserve to experience the best that the human experience has to offer. If not you, then who does? And who gets to decide? As the CEO of your life, the task of travailing pain and purpose to discover pure bliss is unequivocally and undoubtedly yours. You are in charge of your own happiness. It's an inside job that requires self-discovery and an ability to measure personal satisfaction.

I learned early on in my life that carving out time for myself was unquestionable in my personal preservation. While I often gave my all to projects and prospects that I committed to, I learned that in order to consistently show up in this way, I would need to prioritize personal time alone (by myself). I would use my time alone to pray, reflect, rest, and read. It's important to know what fills your cup so that you can be intentional about doing more of it. Take time to search for what feeds your soul and make it a "non-negotiable" in your life. I like to spend my "me time" at the beach or near some sort of body of water. I am comforted by the current and the flow of the water's ripples. It's a reminder to keep moving no matter what chaos or crisis I'm confronted with.

More women should spend time alone. It could be stealing time at the break of day or carving out time during the week that you can dedicate specifically to doing absolutely and only what brings you a sense of peace. Being away from the noise and constant chatter of everyday life really forces you to question how you are fulfilled in the absence of others. Without the influence of outside forces, who are you really? When you're not being ruled by roles and responsibilities, what is it that you need in order to thrive? What are you most afraid of or inspired by?

For me, it's being able to navigate life's journey with continued learning. Seeking out and discovering wisdom is food to my soul and a compass for my future.

Some of the detriments and saboteurs of joy are comparison, fear of failure, procrastination, listening to your inner critic, being unable to forgive yourself or others, attempting to maintain control over everything, saying yes to things that deserve a no, being a perfectionist, having unrealistic expectations, and giving energy to one-sided relationships.

Truly happy people harness the power of forgiveness, they learn from their mistakes, they are able to express gratitude for the good, bad and the indifferent things in their lives. They don't compete with others because they know that they are in a league of their own and that the road to destiny is a marathon and not a sprint. They give themselves room to fail, and they don't take failure to heart or success to the head. They know what they love, and they prioritize both self and soul care. They have a definition of success that amplifies their spirit and not just their bank accounts.

If you live a life of accomplishment and then you go home and feel empty at the end of the day, are you successful? Satisfied? Or content? Success is defined by your ability to visualize a worthwhile goal and then materialize it. So, what happens when you set out to earn more money, buy more jewelry, drive the most expensive car, eat at the fanciest restaurants, or earn the corner office, and then finally achieve it? Sure, most of the world looking in from the outside will attest that you are, indeed, society's definition of success, but what do you do when it doesn't feel that way? How do you respond when you've hit all of your targets and none of them grant you the edified emotion that you expected—when you are faced with the truth that material possessions aren't the most gratifying grace? Do you consider yourself a complete and utter failure? Of course not! After all, you achieved what you believed would be worthwhile; only, perhaps you're in a season of your life that is pushing you to set your sights on things that stir up the most sacred parts of you.

It's important to know that it is unrealistic to expect to be happy all the time. Happiness, like every other emotion, is fleeting, cyclical, ever-changing and ever-evolving. Emotions are meant to move through us. By design, they are an inner manifestation of how we experience life as we stay in motion and move through it. No emotion is permanent. We are meant to feel the emotion and then allow it to pass through us, making room for the next one. When we resist the discomfort of pain, fear, disappointment, grief, loss, rejection, failure, betrayal or anger, we allow prolonged negative feelings to linger. Instead, practice feeling the emotion and releasing it so that it can create space for feelings of joy, excitement, peace, love, acceptance, gratitude, appreciation, and self-worth.

Take a moment to reflect and assess where you are in life and what you want.

1. If you could have anything that you wanted in your life, what would you pursue?

_____

_____

_____

_____

_____

_____

_____

_____

_____

_____

_____

_____

_____

_____

2. When you reflect on childhood memories, what were your happiest moments? Why?

_____

_____

_____

_____

_____

_____

_____

_____

3. How can you recreate or model that same child-like bliss in your life today?

_____

_____

_____

_____

_____

_____

_____

_____

4. When you were a kid what did you want to be? Why?

_____

_____

_____

_____

_____

_____

_____

_____

5. When you anticipate your future, what is it that you hope will happen? What moments and milestones do you have to look forward to?

_____

_____

_____

_____

_____

_____

_____

_____

Chapter 7

STRETCH
Abandoning Your Comfort Zone

———————— • ✳ • ————————

"Dreams often come a size too big so
that you can grow into them, don't
shrink back, STRETCH!"
~Josie Bissett

Stretching requires you to step out on faith, believing that whatever the outcome, God's will for your life will prevail. I can recall being in a room full of women whose businesses averaged up to 100 million dollars in revenue. I remember being asked how it felt to be the lowest earner in the room. At the time my earnings were at the 10 million dollar mark, and while my numbers weren't too shabby, my counterparts had earned up to ten times more than I had. I was taken aback by the question because the way I saw it, merely being in the room was an accomplishment that I was honored to experience. Had I been the highest earner, the most accomplished, or the smartest person in the room, I would have had no capacity to grow. When I saw the earning potential of the other women, it ignited a sense of inspiration within me. I was extremely proud of myself for what I had earned, and there were 990 million reasons why I would continue to strive forward, learn and grow.

Bishop T.D. Jakes once said, "being the best in the room will feed your ego, but it will starve your resources." In order to thrive, you must be exposed to those who are bigger, better, and more accomplished than you are. It's about having access to spaces where there is room for you to stretch into a more advanced version of yourself. Stretching requires getting used to the discomfort of charting into the unknown and coming face to face with the fears that accompany unfamiliarity. Stretching will force you to battle the barriers that keep you beneath massive potential. Stretching will sometimes mean that you have to confront your own ego and finally work through your insecurities, limiting beliefs, and scarcity mindset. These are the very things that cause you to focus on whether or not you are the largest, smallest, or most profitable in a room, completely overlooking the gift of simply being in the room in the first place.

What really counts, is making contact and building genuine connections with the people in the room. As the saying goes, "Your network is your net worth." You are one relationship, and even perhaps one person away from your next big breakthrough. A lot of people think money is always the only means to satisfaction, but it's simply not true. Money is merely a medium of exchange. It does not make you who you are, it only maximizes who you already were.

I remember the feeling of nostalgia, content, and pride when I was awarded a 50 million dollar contract for the first time. As I sat in reflection, I realized that as I acquired higher value contracts, the caliber of my work, my capacity, my strategy for success as well as the people I hired to help facilitate each project all expanded. At each new level of success there was increased effort, insight, experience and wisdom. Each time I leveled up, I applied everything that I had learned to catapult me towards even greater *wins!* Although I had experienced a series of wins ranging from $30,000 to 7 million dollar contracts and so forth, it was the acquisition of the 50 million dollar contract that acted as a defining moment in my life and career.

Having an effective strategy at each level is key when growing a multi-million-dollar firm. You must *pivot* at each level of growth. From my smallest contract award at $30,000, to my largest award at 50 million dollars, what I've found is that growth requires strategy and the ability to learn at the same time.

Leveling UP for the WIN!

Each time that I leveled up to pursue an increased award amount, I activated a higher version of myself. When I increased my effort, my results increased as well.

Getting to Six Figures

I can remember my first $250,000. I had to not only sell myself as the Project Manager, but I also had to find a partner who trusted me and would allow me to act as a subcontractor. I had nurtured a relationship with the

National Institutes of Health, and I developed a strategic marketing plan for their company. I was in search of a partner who had the necessary certifications for the job and would be able to act as a 50/50 partner. When I acquired a partner, it was a seamless yes, on their part. I had already cultivated the deal, developed the relationship, and created the marketing plan. We went on to win the contract, and I sat in the subcontractor/consultant position. Before I could relish in the accomplishment, the excitement of winning the contract was stripped away from me. My partner let me down and kept 75 percent of the contract revenue, leaving me with 25 percent instead of the 50 percent that we had agreed upon. I was undercut my fair share of the deal.

I was so caught up in negotiating the contract, and trusting the referred partner, that I failed to negotiate my own split on paper prior to the award. The lesson in this particular loss was the awareness that at every level you must negotiate on the front and back end. Don't rely solely on verbal agreements. Be sure to back all verbal agreements with legally binding contracts.

Earning the First Million Dollar Rank

I can remember being awarded my first 1.4 million dollar and 3 million dollar deals. My strategy at this level was positioning my team members as 1099 consultants because I didn't have payroll yet. As the owner, contract manager, and project manager all in one, this was the hustle mentality and the act of "betting on myself" to get the job or contract. I leaned heavily on my past relationships at old firms that I had been affiliated with since they knew my worth.

During financial forecasting, I was able to show the bank the current deals I was pursuing in order to secure the necessary capital required to manage the deals.

Although it did not get me additional funding with those particular deals, it did put me on their radar, which would prove to be beneficial later on. Not receiving the funding could be perceived as a failure, but in fact, it was a winning experience. It gave me insight on how to package my pitch to the bank in ways that were more appealing, and it allowed me to further cultivate my relationship with the decision makers, and yet learn where I had fallen short.

This gave me the unique opportunity to come back better the next time.

Getting to 10 Million Dollar Awards

At this level, I transitioned my team from consultant and 1099 status to W-2 employees. This included a full payroll with employee benefits.

I was able to receive an increased line of credit from the bank, which allowed me to bid on higher value contracts.

By this time, I had improved teaming/partnership agreements that were executed by my attorneys. I had everything to gain and nothing to lose. My contract splits honored my worth, and work felt more gratifying. I was now more fulfilled by my work since my improved contract practices allowed me to walk away with the revenue that I earned and deserved. I was finally able to fully leverage the deals that I developed, cultivated, and brought to the table. I was no longer settling for the crumbs; I had earned my keeps for the whole pie.

Getting to 50 Million Dollar Mega Deals

This level required high touch relationship development. I spent three years building a relationship with the agency. I focused on educating myself on the Three C's: Capability, Customer and Competitor.

When I received the Request For Proposal (RFP) for the deal, I took it to the bank board of directors for funding advice. I decided to go the extra mile by researching the bank's decision makers, and I reached out to schedule a meeting with them directly. It was critical that they understood the magnitude of the deal as well as my unique selling proposition. This deal required a $1,000,000 line of credit in order to submit a bid on the contract, and I wanted to speak with those who had the capacity to give me the "yes" that I was seeking.

Further, it was just as important that my partners were a great fit. They needed to be able to meet the requirements outlined in the RFP that I absolutely could not fulfill. I needed to be able to trust them, and they needed to trust me in return. Trust and integrity were a focal point at this level. When pitching to the bank, I was able to build trust through my past performance.

I also needed to become laser-focused. This was the "Mega-Deal," and it required my undivided attention.

I set forth non-negotiable terms immediately following the release of the RFP. I required my potential partners to work with me exclusively, giving them only forty-eight hours to accept or deny my proposition for partnership. I knew it could be a longshot, but I had been intentional on structuring the deal in a way that would make it hard for them to say no. I had purposely selected partners who I knew would represent a win-win scenario. Although this was another bold expression of "betting on myself," I was confident that my pitch was mutually beneficial. Winning on this level wouldn't be self-serving. It would require a collective effort and would present itself as a major win for all involved. When your wins impact the lives of others, this is a sure indicator that you are indeed *Winning on another level.*

When I initially pursued this "mega-deal," I had never bid on a project of that magnitude. Perhaps it was being in the room with women who were shattering the ceilings of earning limits and acquiring 8- and 9-figure deals. I had a refreshed confidence in my potential, but it was definitely something that I would have to stretch for in order to reach, and I was okay with that.

There was something deep inside of me that wanted to know just how far I could go, how big I could really play, how much I could really win. I was determined to unveil the answers to these questions. I was learning myself and becoming more aware of my potential every day.

Sometimes we fail to pursue "God-sized" goals because we focus too much on our limits rather than our potential. When I submitted my team's proposal on the 50 million dollar contract, I knew that we didn't meet all of the requirements necessary to obtain a contract of that proportion, but instead of giving energy to ideas of lack, I focused on what I did have. I had a hyper-engaged, completely competent, and efficient team that was always willing to step up to the plate with me. So, for almost three years, my team and I conducted careful research regarding the project's scope of work, and we gathered intel on whatever we thought would best prepare us for the deal.

When it was time to submit our RFP response, we still didn't have the capacity to satisfy the needs of the contract requirements. But because I had conducted the research and mentally walked myself through the process several times, I somehow felt empowered and willing to bet on myself in a major way. I chose to take the risk of failing miserably with unrelenting confidence in my ability to execute in excellence; this job was totally outside of my zone of comfort, but I was in a place in my life where I no longer wanted to live within the comfort of playing small. My comfort zone had become a cage and not only was I ready to sing, but I was ready to break out and fly. This goal was not within my immediate reach, but I was committed to stretching out my hands in order to challenge myself on a new level.

Again, at the time, one of the contract's requirements was to have a $1,000,000 line of credit. This capital was needed to cover the cost of payroll, operational expenses, as well as other financial obligations until the project paid out. In an inspired attempt to give myself a fighting chance to successfully acquire and deliver on the bid at hand, we considered all possible options. One of the first things that I did was research the leadership team and the board of directors of the bank that was offering the line of credit. I asked bank tellers for information about their knowledgeable staff, and I also researched information online to educate myself on who I would be dealing with. It was important for me to learn the details of who occupied what positions, the culture of the company and the structure of the organization's decision-making process.

In order to secure the loan, I presented documentation that showcased our past performance. Our track record of wins coupled with our company's reputation as it was outlined on paper allowed me to receive the $1,000,000 line of credit that I needed in order to contend in the 50 million dollar arena. I was raising the standard on my personal performance, and I was playing to win; it was the only thing I would give thought and attention to. Losing was simply not a feasible option. I was competing against myself and playing by my own set of rules. I had secured a $1,000,000 credit line prior to even propositioning the partner; this was unheard of. I dared to do something different in order to win like I never had before. You know, it's not every day that a black woman is awarded a million-dollar line of credit, but I had God, grace, and grit on my side. There were no limits to what was possible.

I knew that in order to win, I needed to call large business partners and other supporting roles into play and into focus. I had done extensive research on my competition to see how I would be able to set myself apart from them and also determine who would be the best businesses to bring on as partners. I was searching for a seal of excellence and a proven history of success. I needed to partner with an entity that had the bandwidth and experience to secure a collective win. We moved forward, and we made a decision to select partners with whom we had previously worked and secured wins satisfactorily. We were intentional in choosing partners who exhibited strength in areas where we lacked the required qualifications. We were strategic, deliberate, and extremely determined.

I did not want to be another typical Washington, D.C. contractor in a situation in which a large company decided to subcontract with many small companies just to get a piece of the pie. I didn't want a slice; in order to be truly satisfied, I needed the whole pie, and I knew that I needed the support of a large business partner to assist in our operational strategy. I was aware that if I were to bid in collaboration with three other small businesses, my chances of winning were far higher than if I bid with just one company. In order to partner with a large business, I needed to clearly communicate my value proposition in order to adequately leverage the opportunity before me.

While I was creating all the rules, I required our large vendors to commit to us exclusively. Deciding to take matters into my own hands, I set forth a mandate that required my potential partners to play by my rules. This arrangement gave them a forty-eight-hour timeframe to respond to my partnership. This was completed prior to moving forward and sharing the RFP. Although this was risky, I had stakes in the game, and I was playing to win. I wanted to ensure that we had the proper commitments in order to guarantee that we could fully leverage the loan and proceed to move forward with responding to the RFP. Learning to be creative and exhausting all options takes courage, tenacity, out-of-the-box thinking, and most importantly, being relentless without being obnoxious. I had committed to a vision larger than myself, and I wasn't going to allow anything to diminish my dreams.

We eventually won the contract, and the acquisition became a staple of my career. I had set a new standard and I was never going to shrink back. Instead, I continued to stretch. I would go on to bid on another 50 million dollar contract, and although it was a project of the same fiscal magnitude, it would require a brand new strategy to win a second time around.

We needed a new game plan, new execution timeline, and a new focus. Six years later, I wondered whether or not we could do it again. It took a year for the RFP to come out. This time, we had more details, many different options, and there were several variants related to the project's scope of work. So, we had to decide on what our new strategy was going to be in order to ensure that we could win the contract. It also meant new turf, new territory, new people, a new contract type, and several legal changes. Everyone was watching and hoping they would win, and they were hoping that we would lose.

With a commitment to continued learning, and in preparation to win another huge contract, we had graduated from the U.S. Small Business Administration's (SBA) 8(a) program and had partnered with another firm to pursue this opportunity. We had been cultivating relationships with mentors and giving back to mentees over the years, which increased our effectiveness and chances of winning.

The competition was just as fierce, if not greater this time around. We had to perform our normal due diligence and present a winning value advantage while also competitively streamlining our overall costs. This process required countless meetings and also maintaining a unified front with the end goal of winning in mind. It was a laborious process; however, it paid off in the end because we won the contract.

Always be willing to work outside of your comfort zone. Stretch yourself. Growth is often accompanied by discomfort, it's almost impossible to grow and stay the same. Embrace the shifts in your life; don't allow your limitations to box you in. Know where you display power deficits and then partner with those who are strong in those areas. Know your strengths and then maximize them.

Dwelling within the dimensions of comfort don't keep you safe; they only keep you small. Dare to do something dramatically different in your life so you can reap the benefits of being bold enough to pursue a new level of greatness. Old ways won't open new doors. In order to achieve on a greater scale, you must abandon your comfort zone and chart out towards larger territory. The beauty and power of transformation exists beyond the limits of what you think you can't do. The truth is that you can do hard things. You can break barriers designed to keep you boxed in. You can heal from divorce, build in a basement, and you can earn as much money as you believe is possible.

Abandon Your Comfort Zone

What limitations are keeping you from taking action in the direction of your dreams?

_____

_____

_____

_____

_____

_____

_____

_____

_____

Take a moment to visualize the life of your dreams. Where are you living? Who are you living with? What does work look like in your life? What about play? Are you married? Traveling?

_____

_____

_____

_____

_____

Finally writing a book or starting a business? What does your bank account look like? What about your savings account? What feeling comes over you when you check your bank account statement? Are you at your ideal weight and fitness goal? Who are the people in your life?

_____

_____

_____

_____

_____

_____

Taking time to reflect on your goals and what you want out of life helps you get one step closer to materializing what you visualize.

_____

_____

_____

_____

_____

In order to leave what's familiar and set out towards the unknown, you will first need to imagine your life, not for what it is, but for what it can be.

Use the space below to write out your life's vision.

Habakkuk 2:2 "…write the vision and make it plain on the tablets, that they may run who reads it."

Write out your vision and then go after your dreams!

_____

_____

_____

_____

_____

Sometimes the comfort that we seek is an escape from chaos. No one can blame you for wanting to prioritize peace in your life, but I caution you to examine if the peace you seek is a search for serenity or some sort of resistance to grow. Growth can be scary, but it's a necessary construct of the human design. You deserve to live a life that encompasses the scope of your highest potential.

When you consider your goals, what are you most afraid of? What are the ideas and limits that are keeping you stuck? Write them out and then find solutions that combat those fears. For instance, if you are afraid to start your business because you feel you aren't business savvy enough, a viable method of resolve may be to enroll in a business class. You could hire a business coach or find a mentor who has experience in the industry that you're looking to get into. No one ever told us that our lives would be void of fear, no matter how ambitious we are. We may never get to completely eradicate the emotion of fear, but we can gain fortitude that allows us to perform in the face of it. Fear and faith both require that you believe in an idea that hasn't happened yet. Why not choose one that reflects the best possible outcome?

Use the chart below to assess where you are in terms of your growth and comfort zones.

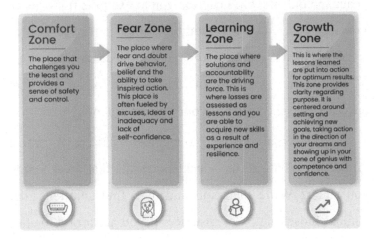

Chapter 8

SHIFT HAPPENS
The Power of the Pivot

————— • ✹ • —————

"A pivot is a change in strategy
without a change in vision."
~Eric Reiss

In the beginning stages of my company, I was on a ferocious journey to discover the limitless possibilities within my potential. There was nothing that I believed I could not do, and I was unapologetically doing it all. Initially I offered multiple services which included:

- Construction Administration

- Space Planning Coordination

- Relocation Planning & Management

- Facilities Operations Support
- Event Planning & Coordination

During that time, a senior official in government contracting, whom I respected greatly, shared with me that over the years, he had witnessed me rise in the ranks, going from an assistant to one of the top project managers in the industry, to business owner. He suggested that I should take a few steps back, scale down, focus on and perfect one particular service offering and then market and manage that, instead of the multi-faceted service tier that we were currently working with.

If his concerned, yet compassionate advice wasn't enough to make me reconsider my service model, to make matters worse, during a presentation, he advised me to focus on a singular sales model, rather than being a Jill of all trades. I was told that I could not be everything, and that I should not attempt to be a master of all trades. This was a hard moment of truth that forced me to take a few steps back and rethink my plan. I had to manage and focus on doing business within one area of expertise as opposed to stretching myself too thin trying to leverage and take on every possible contract in my beginning stages of business.

Never offer too many options to clients that you cannot expertly and adequately provide. I made the decision to focus on one thing and nothing else. The way that I scaled down from offering multiple services to one service was by leading with what I did best. I decided to focus on construction management. I leaned in on my strengths and my prior experiences, and I knew I would be able to eventually expand into other areas. I reduced my company options and chose to return to my foundation. I updated my company essentials to reflect our new service offerings, and I revamped my capability statement.

A capability statement is a one-page document about your company and your services. If your company is a sole proprietorship (meaning it's just you), your capability statement should be about you and your past performance. You must clearly communicate what you're selling to the market and make sure that it's precise and easy to understand. Consider customers for whom you've done work. You want to outline who they are because that shows your credibility. Additionally, consider the skills you've developed, the things you've done well with, and the business partnerships that will provide you with the best references.

You can create a capability statement of your own by answering the Three C's:

- What is your **Capability**? What is it that you're selling?

- Who is your **Customer**? Who are you selling to and what are they buying?

- Who is your **Competitor**? Who can sometimes be your partner? How can you set yourself apart from your competition?

_____

_____

_____

_____

_____

_____

_____

_____

_____

I also changed my business focus by strengthening my past performance relationships and excelling in a single core service. This is how I was able to secure additional contracts. Once I made mastery adjustments, I was ready to increase the services I offered and expand my team even more.

Rethink it, redo it, and reprocess it. When you're trying to determine how to launch your company and move forward, ask yourself, "What is it? What is the one thing that I'm good at?" Also be sure to understand the field in which you are playing. Do the research and understand how to navigate in that field.

Being able to pivot is an indicator of your willingness and openness to explore other possibilities. If living in a global pandemic has taught us anything, it's been to embrace the power of the pivot. Many companies were forced to reimagine their business model, restructure their customer experience, reevaluate their operations, systems, processes, and procedures. Unfortunately, some companies weren't able to withstand the shifts and consequently, we saw many CEOs step down and several businesses both big and small shut down.

There are some changes that come around, and they hit us in our blind spots. Being able to adjust and adapt to unforeseen circumstances could be the difference between a business that figures out how to serve their clients amid chaotic and uncertain conditions, and those who simply close their doors.

Although we've been navigating a worldwide crisis, several organizations have reported increased revenue and customer engagement. This goes to show you that sometimes opposition is an opportunity to do something different, and sometimes it's divine redirection.

You don't show you're a boss by talking about it. You demonstrate your skills through your actions. Real bosses don't have to speak. They execute, and people know who they are by their actions. Be a boss who can get down and do the job. I often have no problem wearing a suit to the board room and steel-toe shoes to the construction site. I'm a boss who is hands on, which I think is most important. Remaining in action, putting in the work, working in the field, and staying connected will always keep you grounded.

When you know your value, honor your worth, and appraise what you bring to the table, you are more empowered to pivot when conditions perpetuate unexpected changes. You can change your method and maintain complete confidence in your mission. Be flexible in your approach and unrelenting in asking for what you know you are worth.

Chapter 9

TAKE ACTION
*The Four Guiding Principles
of Business Growth*

———— • ✹ • ————

*"Take action! An inch of movement
will bring you closer to your goals
than a mile of intention."*
~Steve Maraboli

Core contributors to my success have been inclusive of people, processes and will power. One of the most influential processes that I have employed consistently in establishing and growing my business are the "Four Guiding Principles: Read Up, Show Up, Listen Up, and Follow Up." I learned these principles at a Black Enterprise Conference, and they have helped me to gain substantial research, articulate my vision with levels of confidence, formulate strategies, and benefit from multiple opportunities coming to fruition.

Principle #1: Read Up

Reading is fundamental. I know you probably think it's a cliché message thrown around by your grade school instructors, but it's true. I often read various business magazines including Forbes, Fortune 500, Inc. business journals and various government magazines. Reading helps me to identify market trends, stay in the know of industry updates, research projected issues, and educate myself on the growing demands of business. Reading and staying literate in your industry exposes you to information that you otherwise may not be able to access.

For every opportunity, especially in the government contracting arena, reading has played a pivotal role in the development of my expertise. Committing to continued learning has allowed me to grow in wisdom, stature, and repertoire with my network. I am sought out and hired because of what I know, and I will always be an asset in every room I'm in or anything I'm a part of because I will always challenge myself to learn something new. The best investment that you will ever make is an investment into knowledge.

Principle #2: Show Up

Showing up prepared and in strategic places is critical. I would often show up in places where I knew influencers were. My success in the 8(a) program was a success that was subsequent with simply showing up. I conducted research about who people were, what they did, where they were, and how they could help me. I attended industry events and meetings, and I used the Internet to connect with others and find out where they would be. Moreover, I used strategic alliances and people in my industry to help me identify where these gatekeepers would be located and identify with whom I could connect. As a result of consistent application, we were able to generate significant revenues while in the program.

It's important to know the influencers and identify how you can connect with them. These associations will help you get to the next level and assist you in potentially securing the contract that you desire. For example, I have some new initiatives and goals that I'm working on and I'm repositioning myself the same way I positioned myself years ago. This means that I have to know where the players are, where the action is, and how I can show up.

Principle #3: Listen Up

Gathering information is what listening up is all about. It is important because, regardless of the level that you are on, listening up will ensure that you are able to learn from those with the knowledge, wisdom, and experience of which you are seeking. Think about someone who you have heard speak at a conference or board meeting. Think back to that life-altering message that you received from a mentor, coach, parent or advisor. Do those messages still impact you to this day? This is why listening up is important.

If you're too busy speaking up when you should be absorbing the wisdom, then you may just miss the message. Whenever you enter a new room, come in with your mouth closed but your ears, eyes and mind open. The thing about new levels is that while you may have graduated from where you were before, you are now at the bottom of the totem pole at your new level. This is not the time to try to impress others with what you know, this is the time to check the temperature of the room so that you can become acclimated in your new environment.

Principle #4: Follow Up

Finally, but no less important, following up is as crucial as breathing. In fact, it's often said, *"The fortune is in the follow up."* We often lose out when we don't **follow up**. Eighty-five percent of people simply do not revisit their leads. Their first interaction is often their only interaction, which results in lost opportunities. Following up within the first forty-eight hours is key, and there are various methods that you can use to be successful at this, such as sending an email, making a phone call, or sending a letter. Make sure that you understand your clients and how they prefer for you to follow up with them. All people operate and work differently, so to make this easy, you simply can ask for their preferred method of contact. When you are connecting with others, it's critical to consider why you want to further connect. There's nothing more annoying to a busy person than having their time wasted. When you reach out, remind them where you met, share some insight about the conversation that you may have engaged in. Then it's a good idea to quickly express why you want to connect further and how it can be beneficial to them as well.

Don't allow your first interaction to be your final interaction. Be a part of the 15 percent and take full advantage of opportunities to build connections and leads.

I derive wisdom in many ways from the stance, "The higher the mountain, the thinner the air." This is a sage piece of wisdom that not only helps me to understand the challenges of elevation, but also challenges as they relate to distinguishing effort among people on the way up. I realized that when you're ready to go to the next level of the mountain, people aren't willing to do the things that you do. They want to be on the mountain, but they don't want to endure the climb. They may have sores on their feet, but that's not your worry. Your worry is climbing and getting up the mountain. You must position yourself to go to the next level.

Chapter 10

BE A SMART CEO!
Setting Goals and Hitting Your Target

───────── •✹• ─────────

"Success is hitting your target. Mastery
is knowing that it means nothing if you
can't hit it again and again."
~Sarah Eliza Lewis

Goals activate your vision and allow you to view life with a new pair of eyes. Goals are important because they ensure that you are on a consistent path to development and improvement. They ensure that you are always becoming a better version of yourself. Why does this matter? I'd like to use the idiom, "freshwater flows." Anything that is fresh is always moving and flowing like a stream. If that stream stops flowing and gets backed up, the water becomes stagnant, toxic, and useless.

If you fail to set goals and develop plans for your life, the same will happen to you. You will become stagnant, stale, and stuck. I've found that many people set goals and are unable to follow through on them. To keep myself on track with my goals, I often write out weekly and quarterly to-do lists, and I create an annual vision board. My to-do lists keep me focused, and they help me to hold myself accountable to the things that need my time, attention, and effort. They help me to make sure I stay on target.

In order to use my time effectively, I review my to-do lists daily and visit my calendar weekly to accommodate updates. I also meet with my staff weekly to make sure I am addressing things that we need to tackle. Tracking goals in this manner has allowed me to focus forward and plan ahead. I've "winged it" before, moving forward without a to-do list. The result was invariably that I struggled to accomplish tasks fully, and I did not do well enough to reach my goals with excellence or satisfaction.

To avoid becoming overwhelmed, I set five goals instead of ten. There was a time I said to myself, *I can do it! Let me go for ten. Let me go for the stretch.*

However, I realized that I had placed too much on my plate. As a result, I made the decision not to overextend myself. Instead, I focused on setting attainable goals so I could get a win without sacrificing my peace and sanity. If I stretch to achieve five goals rather than ten, my success rate will be much higher and more feasible, and I will avoid feeling defeated, drained, and burned out.

I encourage you to set five main goals that you want to accomplish over the course of a year. Once you identify your five goals, assess, and decide how you will accomplish those goals over four quarters. Then, focus on what you need to accomplish in the immediate three months. Finally, identify what you need to finish by the end of the week.

Once you do this, you can focus only on that core goal during that quarter. Once you know your goals for the year, break your goals down into quarters, months, and weeks. When you're writing out your to-do list, put action behind it to ensure that you understand your destination and begin with the end in mind. Setting goals and then creating a plan to accomplish them helps you add purpose to your mission. These are the actions that have created success for me and my company.

Goal setting is the development of an action plan designed to motivate and guide a person, an individual, or organization toward a deliberate outcome. Goal setting involves committing thought, emotion, and inspired action towards something worthwhile and ideal.

One of the most prevalent and effective goal setting tools is the SMART goal setting process. SMART goals are: Specific, Measurable, Attainable, Relevant and Time Bound. This system of goal setting helps you to establish clearly defined targets.

The CEO Goal Setting system takes it a bit further. I believe that the SMART tool is incredibly effective. However, it's imperative to imagine how hitting your target will help you to gain Confidence, how it will Empower you, and how it will allow you to feel *On Top of Your Game!*

Having a vision that is inclusive of the social and emotional capital that comes with hitting your target can increase one's will power to push through when they begin to feel discouraged or distracted.

SET YOUR GOALS LIKE A SMART CEO

Goal:

S Specific — What specifically am I trying to achieve?

M Measurable — How will I measure success?

A Attainable — What steps do I need to take to attain the goal?

R Relevant — Is this relevant for my long-term objectives? Is this the right time?

T Time-bound — What is the time frame for the goal?

C Confident — What goals are you able to set with complete confidence? These are the things that are within your realm of brilliance and expertise.

E Empowered — What tools, resources and people do you need in order to maximize your potential? Who adds power to your goals?

O On Top of My Game — List out the outcomes of winning big! Visualize yourself at the top of your game. When you are able to visualize it, you can then materialize it.

Chapter 11

USE WHAT'S
IN YOUR HANDS!

—————————— • ✳ • ——————————

"Do what you can, start where you are,

use what's available."

~Arthur Ashe

How often do we allow the perceived lack of resources to hold us up from taking action towards the things that we want? I can't tell you how many times I've heard people say that they didn't start a project, write their book, launch their business, or implement a great idea because in one way or another, there was something that they thought they needed, and without it, they were powerless. If you've ever felt this way, I encourage you to examine what you do have access to.

I'm a firm believer that we often have access to the tools that we need in order to build a bridge to what's next. Perhaps you don't need a literary agent with notoriety to stamp your book idea. If you don't have access to an agent yet, maybe the next best thing to do is simply begin to put pen to paper. Imagine actually writing the book and then having something substantial to submit to potential agents, rather than a hope and a dream of what you'd like to maybe, hopefully do one day if…

What if I told you that everything required to build where you are was already within your reach? Don't undervalue or overlook your current resources. You could be putting your book writing goals on hold because publishers haven't responded to your Direct Message request to submit your idea. Meanwhile, you haven't even started developing your manuscript, and you are forgetting that your babysitter's mom is a retired editor from the local newspaper. You could be discouraged that no one seems to believe in an idea that you haven't put much effort into. But doesn't it make more sense to start writing the book, and then maybe ask your babysitter's mom if she'd be willing to take on a freelance gig to edit your book?

If you search for an excuse, you will always find one. If you seek out solutions, they will be available to you.

Now that you've created your SMART CEO goals, take a minute to think about what resources you may need to achieve your goals. Think of your network of friends, family, colleagues, community members, peers, mentors, and associates. Think about how those who you are already connected to can potentially assist you with your current needs. What are the resources already readily available to you? A quick Google search, phone call, or email may completely surprise you. Don't give up on your goals because you're spending too much time thinking about what you don't have. Instead, search yourself so you can be aware of the resources that are already in your toolbox.

Use Your Toolkit to Accomplish Your Goals

Assess where you are, what you need, and what you have in order to accomplish your goals. More importantly, aligning your goals with your tools and resources is critical. The many resources available to you include, but are not limited to your personal gifts, college degrees, skills, industry knowledge, different technological platforms, and connections. Don't sleep on any of these because they are critical tools within your reach.

All too often, we tend to discount, discredit, and overlook what we already can access. As a result, we may initially feel as though we are unqualified or unable to reach specific goals. This is when you need to evaluate your toolbox and determine whether the skill sets and knowledge that you already possess within your arsenal are sufficient enough to hit your next target.

In order to reach many of my business goals, I had to assess my toolkit and leverage my relationships. Certifications became a vital part of my company's toolkit because they were necessary for me to reach my business goals and were critical drivers to ELOCEN's success. Keep in mind that we understood that our certifications were tools. What was vital was knowing how to use the tools effectively. This knowledge allowed us to leverage much more in business than those who possessed the same tools but lacked the understanding and awareness of their usefulness.

Many people think that it's possible to move past "Go" or that they will magically elevate to the next level.

Getting to the next level isn't always about having something new; it's about identifying the devices already in your possession and utilizing them to the best of your ability to propel yourself forward.

Let's assess your toolkit. Here are three questions for you to consider:

1. What skill sets and relationships do you currently have?

2. What tools are required for you to reach your goals?

3. When you set your goals, how do you use the tools in your toolbox?

Leveraging your toolkit will allow you to work smarter, not harder and will propel you much more quickly towards your goals.

CEO TOOLBOX CHECKLIST

Create a checklist to identify who you know, it should include a section for how they can help you, and how it may benefit them.

Then take it a step further and outline your skills, strengths, certifications, and anything else of value.

○   _____

○   _____

○   _____

○   _____

○   _____

○   _____

○   _____

○   _____

○   _____

○   _____

Chapter 12

PRACTICE AND
PERFECT YOUR PROCESSES
AND PROCEDURES

———— • ✹ • ————

"Measurement is the first step that leads
to control and eventually to
improvement. If you can't measure
something, you can't understand it. If
you can't understand it, you can't
control it, if you can't control it, you
can't improve it."
~ H. James Herrington

If when you pose the question, "Who knows your company the best?" If your answer isn't "me," then you have a huge problem on your hands. You should always be your own best business and brand ambassador. Although we learn to delegate and rely on our teams and supporting staff, as the executive leader, you should be knowledgeable of the various roles and responsibilities throughout your organization. It may not be in the best interest of your time to perform each role, but you should be clear of the expected outcome of each.

With clarity around the desired end result, the goal is to then hire the right people who are able to operate in each capacity with excellence. Finding the right people to do the things you cannot do is necessary, but this does not absolve you of knowing the ins and outs of your day-to-day operations. Learn ways that you can set yourself apart from your competitors. Being able to identify gaps and differences will empower you to communicate your company's offerings confidently, which will increase credibility and client comfort. Knowing every aspect of your business including minute details is key.

Data is an integral part of your business that you can and should use to measure your company metrics. Data analytics can help you to reflect on peak performance, determine your growth, assess the mistakes that you've made, and identify the successes that you've achieved. While building my company, I would write everything down. I was very intentional and consistent with documenting information and collecting data. This documentation, collection, and review process was how we created our procedures and captured content. I've written every single thing down from Day 1, and I've trained my staff to do the same thing.

I've frequently referred back to the data that we've collected over the years. I use this collection of notes as a reference point, and I repurpose the information and the content. In my company, we have collected data in every department including human resources, accounting, and program operations for our contracts. Even now, we utilize data as I am writing this book. Over the last fifteen or twenty years, I have become more interested in writing a book (the very one you're reading now), and I have collected data going back a minimum of ten years including books, papers, and notebooks containing information that I wanted to share in this body of work.

Once you organize and properly interpret your business data, it will develop into your Standard Operating

Procedures (SOPs), which are a set of step-by-step instructions compiled by an organization to help employees and team members to carry out routine operations. This way, when you expand your team, they will understand and comprehend the steps they should take to accomplish each task.

Delegation/Hiring

As a business owner, there were things that I didn't understand, such as accounting and human resources. I had to work through the logistics of learning those departments and find people who could help educate me in those areas. As a business owner, you will not know all of the avenues, departments, or things that it takes to run a business. But, what's important is that you hire the people who are skilled in the areas in which you are not as strong.

One of the biggest mistakes I made in the beginning was trying to do everything myself. When you try to do it all, it can often put you in a bad situation, and you can lose out. For example, I once had an opportunity on a contract in which I was trying to do everything myself. I was busy being a super project manager *and* the company owner rather than delegating the process. In that situation, I actually lost money on the contract. My attempt at being a one-woman show almost cost me the entire contract until I made the decision to delegate some of the responsibilities.

People don't manage their processes and procedures consistently, but they're always trying to reinvent the wheel. This causes double work, and this can be avoided. Simply work with what you have. I use the knowledge and skills I developed when I was working for other companies, but I consistently manage the processes and procedures because they are repeatable and have proven to be effective.

Work the System

Systems are invaluable. Managementhelp.org defines a system as an organized collection of parts that are integrated to accomplish an overall goal. Every repeated process in each department should be implemented into a workable system. From invoices to hiring, accounting practices, and simply managing projects and clients, documenting, and creating systems has contributed to our success. If you do something more than three times, you need a documented system for it. Without documented processes, you will have chaos, and it will be difficult for your company to grow.

By trade, I am a project manager, and I am process-driven both personally and professionally. I understand the value of having clearly outlined procedures, and I integrate systems and operations as milestones and benchmarks for my team. When you are building with intention to scale, be sure to package your documented procedures and organize them. This is vital because as you begin to build your team, you can train them with ease and efficiency.

Documenting my company's processes and procedures and working the system has helped me to have excellent customer service with my clients, develop stellar contracts, secure repeat business and referrals, and eliminate chaos and errors. People do business with people whom they trust, like, and know. What we often don't realize in business is that repeat business comes from excellent customer service. Make sure that you're developing the relationship with your new customer or client from the onset and that you are checking in as part of your process and procedures. Excellent customer service will ensure that you have repeat clientele.

Inconsistency creates chaos, turmoil, and distractions, which opens a path for negative energy to come into your business. Consistency in implementing systems is of the utmost importance. Creating and implementing processes and procedures are critical, but they are of no value if they aren't implemented regularly.

The objective is to increase efficiency, quality output and uniformity of performance, while simultaneously reducing miscommunication and failure to comply with industry standards and regulations.

While your company SOPs act as a guide for day-to-day functioning, they are way more than "how-to" guides for your team. Your SOPs are the glue that increases cohesiveness for all of the moving parts in your business. They allow the business to run smoothly and set guidelines on delegation, establishing standards for best practices while maintaining consistency.

Consider the functions of your organization: What are the internal processes? What is the client or customer experience? What is the standard of engagement? Take note of how your company can operate in excellence by establishing or revising your SOPs. Use the following template and prompts to get started.

Add Logo Here

Standard Operating Procedure

Title: **Insert Title**	Version Number: <#>	Effective Date: **\<DATE\>**	Page 1 of 2

Revision History		
Version No.	**Effective Date**	**Description**

Approved By: **Date:**

_____   _____

INSERT NAME AND TITLE
HERE, Signature above

1 Purpose

Instructions: Include a simple statement regarding why you are writing this document. It may also be helpful to describe the purpose of the subject matter in the SOP.

2 Scope

Instructions: This describes to whom or under what circumstances (or both) the document applies.

3 Definitions/Acronyms

Instructions: If the definition is standard (accepted throughout the industry) and published, cite the publication (or website).

3.1   First term: Definition of first term. (Citation, if applicable)

3.2   Second term: Definition of second term. (Citation, if applicable)

4 Procedures

4.1   Heading 2

4.2   Heading 2

- Example bullets

- Example bullets

    4.1.1   Heading 3

        4.1.1.1   Heading 4

5 References

Instructions: List all citations and references to other documents/tools. If none, include "None" herein.

6 Appendices

Instructions: Use appendices sparingly. If forms or other items are included as appendices, consider identifying them as EXAMPLES if it is acceptable to edit them when they are used. If no appendices are included, delete this section.

(Visit www.ceonecole.com to download this template and other resources.)

Chapter 13

IMPACT, INFLUENCE & INCOME

————— • ✵ • —————

"Don't ever let anyone count you out,
God chooses who He wants to use."
~Pastor John Jenkins

If you have been living anywhere other than under a rock over the last decade, then you've noticed the rapid increase and integration of technology as well as social media in our societal structure. We are living in a world with intergenerational tweets, Facebook shares and Instagram mentions. Everyone from toddlers to elders use some sort of digital device or social media platform to communicate with others, entertain themselves or seek out information. In a world that is highly dependent on capturing and leveraging attention, there's a reason why marketing agencies are able to charge astronomical prices for advertisements. The truth of the matter is that attention is both currency and a commodity. Entrepreneurs are often affected by shifts and trends in the world; changes in the world often directly impact the economy, so in order to sustain business, entrepreneurs must pay attention to pivots. Entrepreneurs are the problem solvers of the world, so it is in their best interest to forecast potential issues in order to prepare for profit gains or even losses. There is no denying the fact that businesses not leveraging the profit potential of having a digital footprint are leaving major money on the table.

When I first began my journey into entrepreneurship, making money was a primary goal. However, while I was focused on generating revenue, there was something more meaningful. At the foundation of my ambition was a desire to make an impact; to leave the world and the individuals that I was able to interact and engage with better in some way. I sought to make a positive difference in the lives of others. I wanted my life to be an example of what was possible when you believe big and play bigger.

The terms "impact" and "influence" can appear to be directly correlated. Impact is the ability to have a strong effect on the perception, perspective, beliefs, and behaviors of others. While influence is the level of effect that one may have in persuading decisions, when it comes to profitability, both are valuable. When an individual or company is impactful, they are able to measure the ways in which they effect change. When a person is influential, those metrics are determined by conversions. Are you able to contribute to transformation in the lives of others through their business, bank account, or mindset? Remember, people are often inspired by stories, but they invest in solutions that they believe will enhance their lives in one way or another.

Corporations have been able to quantify the influence and impact of stakeholders, board members, and employees using what is called an influence/impact matrix. This tool helps to determine which stakeholders have the most influence and the impact they can make on future project or company success.

According to an article published by Puneet Kuthialia, a project management consultant and author of

Project Management Battlefield, stakeholders are mapped for their influence and impact on the project in this model. This shareholder classification is essential to determine their information needs and to communicate effectively with them. Their influence, (amount of involvement) and the impact (ability to effect change) are critical to the project's planning and execution.

This tool assesses stakeholders' influence and impact. The amount of influence or impact is divided into two broad categories as low and high. This, then, creates four categories into which a stakeholder can be classified.

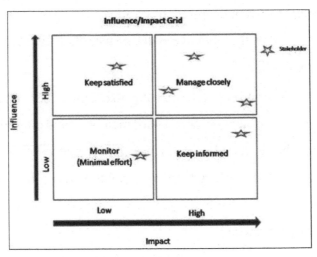

Use the grid to assess your personal influence and impact as well as the members of your team.

The most important group to the Project Manager is the individual with the highest involvement with your project and the highest impact affecting changes in your plans or the execution of the project. You must involve them with details of your project progress and seek their potential impact in making the necessary mid-course corrections, if necessary. Therefore, your priority during mapping of stakeholders should be to identify the persons who are movers and shakers as soon as possible and get them involved into your project.

Next, there are those who have high levels of involvement or influence yet lower level of impact and those with low levels of involvement, but a substantially higher degree of impact. Both these groups must be kept satisfied in their information needs, to keep them on the right side and get help when the need arises. The fourth group, low influence, and low impact needs, requires only monitoring to see if any communication needs arise. Otherwise, it is the least effort map zone.

When you start classifying stakeholders, place them on the grid based on the assessment of influence and impact as shown by the star icons on the image. These mappings are qualitative rather than quantitative. When this mapping exercise is complete, it'll clearly indicate the stakeholders that need most of your attention.

Chapter 14

CEO SOUL CARE
*Prioritizing Peace
and Wellness in your Life*

——————— • ✸ • • ———————

*"Go in the direction of where your
peace is coming from."*
~ C. Joybell C.

Growth is a journey of learning and unlearning. It's an individual odyssey of self-discovery, self-awareness, and personal preservation. This truth can be applied to all facets of life. When we become better in our personal lives, growth becomes evident in our businesses, in our relationships, and in the way we show up in the world.

As I sit, now and reflect on the things that are most important to me, I can honestly say that both my values and beliefs have to shifted throughout the decades. These types of transitions are necessary; as you grow wiser, your perspective will shift to match the level that you are on. In this season of my life, peace is my main priority. When I launched my business in my thirties, profitability may have been my priority. We determine the hierarchy of our priorities based on our needs and the things that fulfill us. I determine what's most important to me based on the things that best align with my core values. Although every business owner must focus on profit potential, I've grown to learn that peace is the real prize. When there is harmony in our lives, we are able to make better decisions, execute on our ideas, and operate in clarity. These things subsequently result in increased abundance.

High achievers often possess an intrinsic gift to perform well under pressure and execute during chaos. Yet, while it is admirable to be able to push yourself to the limit in the name of the grind, burnout and mental exhaustion are not prizes worth winning. I've decided to abandon the hustle in order to adopt the flow. At this point in my life and career, "flow" is the result of building a solid foundation, of developing and implementing effective systems, operations, and procedures. Other contributors to flow are having a proven business, a strong brand promise, and successfully protecting my company and personal reputation by always operating in integrity and excellence.

Now that I've been an adequate funnel, business can now flow to me. I believe in hard work, but I understand that peace is priceless. When I started prioritizing wellness in my life, my worth increased. I started treating myself as someone of value and the world took notice. I gave up people pleasing, and I only committed to things that were within my capacity. I no longer overextend myself, overcompensate in relationships, or help others at the cost of my own wellness. Once I learned to say no, my peace increased.

Take some time to develop your own CEO Soul Care routine. This daily routine should be your compass for optimal living. You must be clear about what you need in order to function at your highest and best potential.

This means developing and asserting healthy boundaries, implementing a healthy diet, and adopting a healthy lifestyle. How much sleep do you need in order to exhibit peak performance? What inspires you? What drains you? How much water do you intake daily? When was your last health checkup?

Create a non-negotiable CEO Soul Care routine.

_____

_____

_____

_____

_____

_____

What boundaries do you need to assert?

_____

_____

_____

_____

_____

_____

_____

What do you need to do more of? When are you at your best?

_____

_____

_____

_____

_____

_____

_____

_____

_____

_____

Once you start to prioritize your wellness, your performance level increases in other areas of your life. Now that you have created your own CEO Soul Care Routine, I want you to extend the work by also focusing on your mental and physical fitness. Below is an exercise plan that one of my mentees, Jessica Laine, developed after shadowing me and noticing the correlation between my mood and my performance. This is a fun exercise that helps you to strengthen both your mind and your body.

CEO NECOLE'S WORK-OUT PLAN

<u>Rules:</u>

1. Pick one word from the "Word Bank" below based on your current mood.

2. Use the alphabet key to spell out your word. Each letter represents an exercise.

3. A word cannot be repeated until other words are complete.

4. Two to three sets of everything.

5. Once you start you cannot stop.

6. No more than one minute break in between each set. (Set a timer!)

<u>Word Bank:</u>

<u>On Track</u>	<u>Focused</u>	<u>OFF Track</u>
Confident	Achieve	Determination
Happy	Accomplish	Perseverance
Blessed	Visionary	Endurance
Successful	Goals	Commitment
Loved	Strategist	Encouragement

Alphabet Key:

A. One-minute plank

B. Fifteen jump lunges on both sides

C. Twenty step ups on each leg

D. Fifty high knees

E. One-minute mountain climber

F. Fifteen stationary lunges on both sides

G. One-mile run

H. One-minute wall sit

I. Twenty-five plank jacks

J. Twenty-five sit ups

K. Twenty-five 25 crunches

L. Twenty-five curtsy lunges on both sides

M. Twenty-five squats with a three second hold between

N. Twenty-five standing oblique twists

O. Fifteen push ups

P. Fifteen alternating lunges on both legs

Q. Twenty-five squats

R. Twenty-five Russian twists on both sides

S. Fifty jumping jacks

T. Fifteen burpees

U. Fifteen inch worms

V. Twenty-five jump squats

W. Thirty shoulder top planks

X. Fifteen tricep dips

Y. Twenty-five bicycle abs

Z. Twenty-five leg drops on both sides

Chapter 15

THE ART OF FAILING UP

———— • ✴ • ————

"You may encounter many defeats,
but you must not be defeated. In fact, it
may be necessary to encounter the
defeats, so you can know who you are,
what you can rise from, how you can
still come out of it."
~Maya Angelou

Sometimes people think that I've accomplished success overnight, but in fact, the journey to where I am now has spanned across my lifetime. You see, there is no "Overnight Success." Success is a series of long nights, early mornings, failures, losses, learned lessons, and momentous moments that force you to level up. Failures have contributed more to my success than any accomplishment or award. There is a wealth of wisdom to be extracted from what you do wrong and in areas where you fall short. I know that within my failures, I have experienced monumental growth. When I think about failure, one person who has inspired me most is Michael Jordan. Many people look at him and say, "Wow, he's successful! He's wonderful! He's on top of the world!" However, they don't know what happened in the dark or his struggles with failure.

As an entrepreneur and athlete, he's had thousands of failures to precede his widespread success. He's had plenty of missed shots, layups, thousands of missed slam dunks. However, in those failures, he made the necessary adjustments to improve his craft. He took those failures and turned them into fires.

Now, I simply view failures as challenges that will stretch me to greater heights, even if I seem to stumble upon them. You don't know when failure is coming, and you don't know when success is coming. You may not go out looking to fail, but you certainly will encounter failures and disappointments when you least expect them. Success and failure simply go hand in hand. If you find someone who is not making mistakes, it's most likely that they aren't challenging themselves. Success is just failure turned inside out. We often desire success, but we don't want to experience the sting of failure. But much like tragedy and triumph, and even pain and purpose, you often cannot experience one without first being exposed to the other.

There are two things that I've learned in the midst of failure:

1. I learned from my pastor that when failure arrives, a breakthrough is near.

2. When people encounter failure, they tend to shut down because they're trying to solve the problem immediately and without support. You must pace yourself and take the journey one moment and one step at a time. Reflect on it, analyze it, focus on it, and seek out solutions. Rely on the support of your network. Your progress will be directly impacted by the people around you.

Initially, I was extremely scared of failing in my business, and my fear of failure hindered me from going out into the market. I would defeat myself mentally with thoughts such as, *I'm not large enough to bid on a job with larger companies. I need to stay within a certain realm or a certain price point.*

However, I don't make decisions through the scope of inadequacy, lack, or fear anymore. I realized that the larger companies prepared just like I could prepare, and I took it one step at a time. I don't worry about how I'm going to tackle the next thing because I know that I have to get through the first thing first. We tend to look at the entire task that we have to accomplish, but we have a series of steps that are required to progress through those tasks. The best way to conquer the tasks without allowing fear of failure to get in the way is to just break the tasks down into small parts and then execute bit by bit.

Remember, everything takes time. Success does not occur overnight. Whether you are experiencing failure or achieving success, you must exercise both patience and diligence at all times.

When you resist failure, you ultimately sabotage your growth. Failures in life may knock you down, but they are not designed to keep you down. Always harness the power to get back up. It doesn't matter how many times you fall; you can always get back up. You can always start again, and you can always rebuild. As long as you have a pulse, God has a plan. Rest in this truth, and know that massive success is your portion.

Don't settle for mediocre ideas or small goals. Go big or stay in bed. I don't mean to be harsh, but if you don't wake up every morning with a vision, you're not making the most out of your time on this earth. Do something that makes you feel alive. Do something that creates opportunities for others. Build something that disrupts systemic oppression and systems that hold back the marginalized and underdeveloped. Reach out and help someone grow,—invest in someone's development and challenge yourself to think beyond your own immediate gratification. This is no time to shrink back, be overlooked in the back of the boardroom, accept disrespect or disregard for the value that you add. What you may have lost was never meant to help you get to your next level. The gateway to what's next in your life is a matter of what you have left…not what you lost.

This is a heartfelt invitation for you to play a bigger game in your life, to lead with integrity and vision, and to build a community of like minds to grow with. This is a clarion call for you to become *Confident, Empowered, and on Top of your Game!*

CEO AFFIRMATIONS

Words have the power to heal, empower, influence growth, and shift one's perspective. When you pursue greatness, words will prove to be one of your greatest weapons. Affirmations are effective because they create a mental image that represents a desired outcome. When you can hold an idea in your head, you are much more likely to take the inspired action necessary in order to hold it in your hand. Being able to *see* the outcome is often a prerequisite to achieving it. So, speak what you seek until you see what you said!

Affirmations have been a valuable tool in my artillery to achieve massive success. Below are my personal CEO declarations and affirmations. Incorporate these powerful words in your self-talk and feel free to add your own to the list.

CEO Affirmations:

1. **God Has No Limits**. I am capable of winning in all areas of my life!

2. **NO = Next Opportunity**. When a door does not open for me, it simply means that it is not my door. I don't doubt my ability to acquire access, I simply move forward to the next door with enthusiasm and expectancy.

3. **Fortune Is In The Follow-Up**! I maximize the opportunities in my life by connecting with others and considering mutual exchanges of value.

4. **I Get To The Bag**! I will not be distracted by things that don't bring me closer to my goals of building wealth. I release thoughts, ideas, and behaviors that fail to serve my greater good. I spend my valuable time focusing on revenue generating activities.

5. **I Am Amazing. I Am Talented**. It's my season. It's my time and my gift is in demand!

6. **I Choose To Win**. I never lose. I either win or learn.

7. **Failure Is Not An Option**.

8. **I Am A Boss**! I am a leader. I make good decisions that positively impact the lives of others.

9. **I Bring My "A-Game" Everyday (Authenticity)!**

I am unapologetically *me*.

10. **Every Day I Earn Respect**. My team respects me, and my community respects me. I am respectable, honorable, and integral.

11. **God Is My Guide.** He makes all of the decisions.

12. **I Am Always Willing To Try**! And when the outcome doesn't meet my expectations, I simply try again!

13. **I Communicate, Collaborate, And Celebrate**. I have people in my life who are happy to see me win. I speak up when I need help, I clap for others when they win!

14. **Revitalize And Recharge**. Rest is a vital part of my self-love and self-preservation process.

15. **I Give Without Expectation**! Charity and tithing are a part of my wealth building strategy. I happily

give to those who can never repay me because I believe in abundance. Whatever I give away makes its way back to me with interest and increase.

16. **I Have Courageous Transparency.** Never fear the opinions of others. I am clear and confident about who I am. I am not swayed by the opinions of others because I am sure about my purpose and my power.

17. **I Stay Flexible—Always Be Willing To Pivot.** Even when I have to change my strategy, I remain committed to my vision.

18. **I Am Comfortable Being Uncomfortable.** Because I Know that my comfort zone doesn't keep me safe. It only keeps me small.

19. **I Am A Student of Life And I Take Notes!** I Am always learning, growing, and evolving. It is my superpower!

20. **I Always Bet On Me! I Am a Winner!** All I do is Win!

When backed with inspired action, our words are transformational declarations that drive us towards our destiny. Another way to activate the power of the spoken word in your life is through prayer. Prayer allows you to have moments of stillness where you focus intently on your desires with hope, expectancy, unrelenting belief, and faith in a divine outcome.

As a high achieving CEO, prayer is one of the most used tactics in my power playbook. It's a sacred time of submission, solitude, and sacred connection with my higher power. It's momentous moments through stillness and reflection that remind me that God is my source, and I have unlimited and unrestricted access to His power. Every CEO needs a personal prayer that covers their vision for the future. Here is mine. Use the section below to write out your own.

CEO Prayer:

Thank you, Lord, for all that you have done in my life and all that you continue to do.

Please provide steadfast guidance and direction on how I can be used as a willing vessel to *lead, guide, instruct, inspire* and *grow!*

With you by my side, *all things are possible!*

Amongst the many tasks and responsibilities before me, it often seems like there's so much to do.

Help me to navigate through it all, alleviating the pain, pressure and stress that comes with the territory of building.

I TRUST YOU LORD, , and I know that you are with me. God cover my business, increase my territory, grant me strategies to build wealth, bless my team, clarify my vision, and expand my reach. Lord, allow me to make a positive impact in the lives of others. When I am weary, restore me. When I am doubtful, remind me of your power. When I am distracted bring me back into focus.

Bless the works of my hands and protect all that I have built.

Amen!

Confident. Empowered. On Top of My Game! ®

Write out your own sacred CEO Prayer!

_____

_____

_____

_____

_____

_____

_____

_____

_____

_____

_____

_____

_____

_____

_____

_____

_____

_____

_____

ABOUT THE AUTHOR
Necole Parker Bio

Necole Parker is an entrepreneur, speaker, philanthropist, and author.

Necole formed The ELOCEN Group, LLC, a Program & Project Management provider of the built environment, in 2007. Under her astute leadership, ELOCEN has secured and successfully completed numerous notable federal, state, local, and commercial projects. Necole guided ELOCEN through the U.S. Small Business Administration's 8(a) Business Development Program, graduating from the program in 2018. Since inception, she has spearheaded the company's successful generation of over 140 million dollars in sales.

Understanding the importance of community involvement, Necole established her non-profit, The ELOCEN Group Foundation (EGF), to serve as an advocacy framework for teen mothers and African-American males raised in single parent households. Through EGF, she has established the "The Jordan McKnight Scholarship Endowment," launched the "$1 Million to Achieve for 1 THOUSAND to Succeed" campaign to provide educational opportunities for children and young adults in underserved communities, and continues to empower communities via community supported events, drives, scholarships, and fundraising campaigns.

Necole holds several Board positions including: Virginia Union University (Board Trustee), Revenue Authority for Prince George's County (Vice-Chair), SHABACH! Ministries, Inc., Walker's Legacy, Capital Region Minority Supplier Development Council (CRMSDC), DC Chamber of Commerce, and The ELOCEN Group Foundation (Chair). In addition to a number of White House invitation visits under the Obama administration, Necole is a U.S. Black Chamber President Circle member, has memberships in various professional organizations, and is the recipient of numerous awards:

<u>AWARDS</u>

- The Daily Record – *2020 Maryland's Top 100 MBEs Award Circle of Excellence Inductee*

- Capital Region Minority Supplier Development Council – *2019 TOP 100 MBEs Award*

- U.S. Black Chambers, Inc. – *2019 Small Business of the Year Award*

- LeadersNest – *2018 FedFem Award*

- Richmond Continental Societies, Inc. – *2018 Champion for Children Award*

- Mid-Atlantic Region – *2017 TOP 100 MBEs Award*

- MD Governor's Citation – *2017 National Women's Small Business Honoree*

- U.S. Small Business Administration – *2016 Woman-Owned Small Business (WOSB) Washington, DC Community Recognition Award*

- Women Business Owners (Prince George's County) – *2015 WBO Pinnacle of Leadership Award*

- U.S. Small Business Administration – *2015 Small Business Person of the Year (Washington, DC) and (National 3rd Place Runner Up Winner)*

- The Daily Record – *2015 Maryland's Top 100 Women Award*

- Mid-Atlantic Region – *2014 TOP 100 MBEs*

- FraserNET Power Networking Conference – *2014 Female Entrepreneur of the Year Award*

- Women Presidents' Organization – *2014-50 Fastest-Growing Women-Owned/Led Companies*

- Enterprising Women – *2014 Enterprising Women of the Year Award*

- Collective Empowerment Group – *2013 Small Business Owner Award*

- 100 Black Men (DC)/WPO – *2013 Women of Color Award*

- Washington Business Journal – *2013 Women Who Mean Business Award*

- DC Chamber of Commerce – *2013 Women in Business Champion of the Year*

- Mid-Atlantic Region – *2012 TOP 100 MBEs*

- American Express OPEN© Victory in Procurement *2012 Woman Contractor of the Year Award*

Necole has also been featured in the following articles:

ARTICLES

- Maryland Daily Record July 2020 – Circle of Excellence Profile

- MediaPlanet.com October 2019 – How SBA is Helping Woman and Minority-Owned Businesses Thrive

- MBE Magazine Cover Article Feature Winter 2016 – *Million Dollar Baby*

- Black Enterprise Magazine Cover Article Feature November 2014 – *Big Companies Accelerate Small Business*

- Featured in Black Enterprise Magazine's March 2014 edition – *Business Breakthroughs*

- Featured in Essence Magazine's February 2014 edition – *Tap Into Your Millionaire Mind-Set*

In 1993, Necole earned a Bachelor of Science in Business Administration from Virginia Union University. She received certificates from the Tuck School of Business at Dartmouth's Building A High-Performing Business Program (2014) and the Tuck–WBENC Executive Program (2013). She is also a certified Facilities Management Professional through the International Facilities Management Association (2018).

To connect with CEO Necole Parker, be sure to visit:

www.ceonecole.com

Connect on Social

Instagram | Twitter | @ceonecole

LinkedIn @necoleparker

Made in the USA
Coppell, TX
12 October 2021